Stand UP
— or —
Bend Over

Financial Knowledge for
Pride, Peace & Power

Thomas Johnson

≋Minuteman **Financial**

Minuteman Financial
P.O. Box 247, Fox Lake, IL 60020
www.standuporbendover.net
tjohnson@standuporbendover.net

Copyright © 2013 by Tom Johnson and Minuteman Financial.
All rights reserved, including the right to reproduce this book
or portions thereof in any form whatsoever.

For information address Minuteman Subsidiary Rights
Department, P.O. Box 247, Fox Lake, IL 60020

Minuteman Financial and Tom Johnson Print Edition.

Visit our website at
www.standuporbendover.net
Email us at: tjohnson@standuporbendover.net

Edited by Frank DiCostanzo
frank@messinamg.com

Cover Design and Content Layout by:
Jeff Whetstone
Elah Strategic Marketing Solutions
www.ElahSolutions.com

Acknowledgement

This book is dedicated to all my clients who have allowed me to be a part of their lives. They have not only allowed me to assist them, but have also challenged me to write this book, allowing me to further use my God-given talents and gifts. This project has filled me with purpose, joy and a great sense of accomplishment.

I know that when you've been talked down, beat down and just plain worn out, it is hard to STAND UP. My clients have allowed me to demonstrate and teach them how to STAND UP. Thank you.

This book has become a reality by the grace of God and by the encouragement, help and support of many people. My wife and family have encouraged and provided honest critiques to keep me on track. The editing team of Ellen and Kathy did a marvelous and timely job. Dawn has always been an inspiration and a cheerleader. Jeff provided so much of the technical support and guidance, as well as hours of conversation, to stimulate the little gray cells and help me recall significant material.

A heartfelt thanks to countless friends and business associates that have been there to stimulate, challenge and take interest. You have all made a great contribution to bringing this book into being.

Thank you and God bless.

Tom Johnson

Purpose

THIS IS FOR MR. & MRS. AMERICA

The purpose of this book is to motivate, inspire and create awareness for you, the reader, as to how you can STAND UP in your daily life.

The financial knowledge you gain in the chapters of this book will EMPOWER you to take action. Your actions will engender PRIDE in what you achieve, and you will gain a PEACE that allows you to function with less stress.

We all need to know that we can STAND UP! And we need to recognize the opportunities we all have to;

- **STAND UP** to overcome fear.

- **STAND UP** because it is necessary and right. It will change your life.

- **STAND UP** and others will stand with you.

- **STAND UP** because you live in a country that allows it.

- **STAND UP** and people will respect you and look up to you.

- **STAND UP** because it improves your view of the situation, the opposition and yourself.

Stand Up or Bend Over

We get caught up in politics–right and left–and lose sight of right and wrong.

We get caught up in political correctness and lose sight of our freedom of speech and our right to express ourselves.

We listen to the media and allow them to form our opinions, rather than thinking it through and forming our own.

We rarely exercise common sense–to think rationally and logically, to draw conclusions based on facts, knowledge and a deeper understanding of the topic or issue.

We allow ourselves to be influenced by others' agendas, biases and ignorance.

We have bought into the concept that "everyone is a winner." That there should be no losers. Yet we all know that is not real life.

Where is the challenge to be all you can be?
Where is the determination to excel and be proud?
Where is the motivation to use your God-given talents to
benefit yourself, mankind and the glory of God?
Where is the opportunity for you to be an inspiration
to someone else?

We all need to STAND UP and make a difference in every aspect of our lives. I suggest the starting place be up close and personal. That is…with YOU!

<u>STAND UP in:</u>
YOUR PERSONAL LIFE.
YOUR PERSONAL RELATIONSHIPS.
YOUR PERSONAL FINANCES.
YOUR JOB.
AS AN AMERICAN AND A HUMAN BEING.

Purpose

When you STAND UP and make a difference, you will begin to establish trust. Trust in yourself (confidence), and trust from others (respect).

In all we do, we constantly strive to engender TRUST. We want people to believe us. This is the essence of what we truly strive for. Within our families, we want their trust. We need to know they believe in us. They, in turn, need to know we can fulfill our promises. They need to know we can provide, protect and love them.

The same is true of our relationships with our employers. Trust is a mutual element of all relationships. Sports teams, political parties, law enforcement, school boards, associations, governments and nations–all require the establishment of trust.

All that is presented in this book is purposed designed to encourage, instruct and motivate the reader to STAND UP–. To achieve your potential by creating trust forof others and, self- respect, and energizinge you to stand taller, reach farther, run faster and enjoy your life to the fullest. To be and do what you were put on this earth for.

Hopefully this book will motivate you and you will share it with others. Be determined to start now to change the rest of your life for the better. Learn from your past. Wake up the inner you and use all you have been given. Develop every dimension of your life–spiritual, relational, vocational, educational and family. Become the whole person you were intended to be.

Half a person is like half a truth. The best part may have been left out.

After reading the book we challenge you to learn more about
Tom Johnson and How to Stand Up in your life at
www.standuporbendover.net

Contents

ACKNOWLEDGEMENT I

PURPOSE III

INTRODUCTION IX

1. COMMON SENSE 1

2. STARTING OVER 7

3. FEAR 15

4. CREDIT 21

5. CONSUMER PROTECTION 35

6. HOW TO STAND UP! 51

CONSUMER BILL OF RIGHTS 78

Please note: blank pages are provided at the end of each chapter for your own notes, so you can personalize this inspirational idea book and make it YOURS.

Stand UP or Bend Over

Financial Knowledge for Pride, Peace & Power

VIII

Introduction

This book is created after thirty-five years of experience counseling people with their personal finances. I have not seen and heard it all, but I don't think I've missed much. I've seen too many clients who were frustrated because they felt defeated, a failure, hopeless. Add to that the common factor that their marriages were suffering due to escalated discussions (arguments) and tremendous guilt.

The title of this book has great meaning in the realm of personal finance. If you don't STAND UP and take responsibility, gain knowledge and apply it, and develop and commit to a strategy to achieve your goals, you might as well just BEND OVER and take the punishment. You will make your creditors smile. And you will lose

This book is written for the common person. I have tried to express everything in plain and simple language. I am not an attorney and I strongly recommend you seek legal counsel for your situation if you feel you might need it. I also strongly recommend you apply common sense while you read and as you begin to apply the principles embedded in this book. You will need to open your mind to new thinking and conduct. Change will probably be necessary, as you cannot expect to get new results without changing your attitude, mindset and actions.

Some things stand out as I reflect on my clients, their plight, their attitudes, their preconceived ideas, their relational stress and their inappropriate decisions with respect to their finances. I want to state clearly one of the cornerstones of my practice to this day: no matter what brought the client my way, there was never any condemnation in my office. Whatever choices they made, or whatever circumstances were beyond their control– whether plain stupidity, an inflated ego or anything else–I would never dwell on it.

And I want to tell you the same thing. You will beat yourself up, and other people will also volunteer to do that. Don't do it to yourself, and don't allow anyone else to do it to you. It's unproductive and a waste of time.

Personal finances affect every dimension of your life. No part of your life escapes the impact of finances. I believe most people want to be good stewards of their money. The question is: How, when and where are you supposed to learn? It's kind of like learning how to raise children. When you can least afford it and you have the least knowledge, and with no experience, you have children. It might be called on-the-job training.

The intent of this book is to begin to equip you with some smarts as to how to do a better job, reduce your level of stress and begin to move toward financial freedom. Unless you had unusual parents, you weren't taught much about managing money. Childhood is over, and you need to think like, act like, and execute your life like a responsible adult. You will not get it by osmosis. And you will not get it unless you commit to learning the principles of budgeting, saving, and setting goals and priorities. You must also be determined to achieve your goals. As an individual or as a couple, you may want to seek out a mentor that will challenge you and help you stay focused. Regardless of what approach you choose, you must acknowledge that you need to make some changes. Determine to give up the way you once thought about money, the way you have consciously and deliberately avoided planning and prioritizing what you do with your money. If you don't think you can do this, then close the book. You might as well continue doing whatever you have been doing and hope for the best.

The material presented in this book is not difficult to understand, and it is not impossible to achieve results. The fact that you are reading this book is probably an admission that you have a financial problem or that you want to improve the way you've been doing business. It's an act of reaching out for help. You will soon make some changes that will create improvement and ultimately financial freedom. These changes will become obvious as you proceed through the pages that follow.

Learning to STAND UP is a process and you will grow into it. Be determined to STAND UP on the inside and say to yourself, "Enough is enough!" Equip yourself with knowledge and with the rules of the game. This means the areas of credit, borrowing, consumer protection, saving, budgeting and more. You can do it! This book is empowering and will always be with you for reference. You can STAND UP when dealing with creditors. When you learn how to stand up for yourself in the financial arena, you may be surprised where else you can STAND UP and make a difference.

You may find additional help at our website, www.standuporbendover.net. There you will find some excellent educational classes. You will also find the book, "**CASH POOR / CREDIT RICH.**" This is an instructional book providing more details to assist you in achieving your goals.

STAND UP AND CHANGE YOUR LIFE!

Chapter 1

Common Sense

A 21ST Century Version

About two hundred and forty years ago, a wise man by the name of Thomas Paine wrote a little book titled "Common Sense." The book seems to have been lost in the shadows of history, its content largely forgotten. As defined by Webster, "common sense" is simply: sound and prudent, but often unsophisticated judgment.

The various thoughts, arguments and ideas that Paine wove together in his "Common Sense" built a case for a revolution. The revolution was the vehicle to freedom and an escape from underneath the thumb of King George. Without a revolution, they might as well have gone back to England. The greatest army and navy the world had known could not dissuade the colonists from a revolution against Mother England.

Stand Up or Bend Over

The common sense that Thomas Paine used and spoke of could be used today and has strong applications in every American's life. To STAND UP and demonstrate that we have common sense would be a unique event in many people's lives.

In this chapter, I want to challenge you to exercise those little gray cells and to begin to apply your God-given common sense.

When was the last time you sat down and did a thoughtful assessment of You? Your life? Your opportunities? Your resources that are wired into you? When did you thoughtfully try to get your head around the challenges you are facing? Have you ever tried to think of the disaster you are faced with as an opportunity? Stand up and admit you need to do this! You and you alone are the only one qualified to do this. For you know more about you than anyone else does. You may need your spouse, a mentor or a trusted friend to be a sounding board. You should use every resource available to you to redirect, restructure and restart your life. Be brutally honest with yourself.

On self-evaluation, most people quickly determine they have been given the short end of the stick. Consider instead: Maybe this is an opportunity. Maybe this is a blessing in disguise. The loss of a job, a broken relationship, you didn't make the team, an injury…these events are life. They happen. They are real. Pick yourself up and move on. How does the song go? "Whenever you're down and out, the only way is up."

"The ultimate measure of a man is not where he stands in moments of comfort and convenience, but where he stands in times of challenge and controversy." – Martin Luther King Jr.*

---

*"Strength to Love," pg. 35

Common Sense

I want to challenge you to expand your mind, enlarge your world, gain a broader perspective and determine to make your life more reasonable, enjoyable and ultimately more successful.

Let me suggest that you think of your life as a thousand-piece puzzle. When you open the package and dump it out on the table, it is a pile of disorganized pieces that appear helter skelter and make no sense. For those of you who have never done a puzzle, I suggest you first begin to organize the pieces. Turn them all face up. Gather the edge pieces. Sort all the pieces by color. Begin looking for little puzzles within the puzzle. Then begin with putting just two pieces together. One piece at a time will keep you moving toward the goal of a completed picture puzzle. You may not know what the finished picture will look like, but it will get clearer as you connect the pieces. You become more and more intimately aware of each detail, eventually completing the beautiful picture by carefully placing one piece at a time. The pieces that didn't relate to anything early on suddenly have a place–they fit–because you can comprehend the total picture. Try to relate this process to putting the pieces of your life together.

The 21st century is full of challenge, frustration, choices and opportunity. We have never had so much to choose from. In the electronic age of cyberspace, online shopping, education, matchmaking, and just about anything else you might think of, are all at your fingertips. Our choices are endless. Life is like going into the super market. the options and the choices we face in the grocery store are unbelievable. The kings of old didn't have nearly the choices that you and I have today, just plain folks. Think about it and let it settle into your mind. You have choices. You are free to choose. Take advantage of it. Don't be overwhelmed by the adversity that has befallen you or the myriad of choices you have to choose from.

Stand Up or Bend Over

You need to connect the dots in your life and to begin to make sense out of it. COMMON SENSE! Open your mind to the opportunities all around you.

I often ask my clients a series of questions. If you had total freedom to choose, what you would do for the rest of your life? What would you choose? What would energize you, rather than exhaust you? What would provide satisfaction and make you feel that you had a purpose in life? What would it be?

Too many people look at me like deers caught in the headlights and don't have a clue how to answer. They have never thought about it. No one has ever challenged them to try this thought-provoking, mental gymnastic activity. I dare you to try it. Once you have made a breakthrough, you will never turn back.

When you really grasp the concept and begin to gain insight into yourself, your perspective of yourself and your world will be forever changed. When you begin to direct or take charge of your life in this manner, you will experience new dimensions in your relationships, your job, your attitude, your willingness to change and much more.

This will overflow into every dimension of your life. How you see change and opportunity. How you can embrace change, rather than fight it or flee from it.

I believe your life will be affected to such a degree that you will handle relationships better and begin moving toward your hopes and dreams. You will take time to think about goals and those dreams you once thought impossible.

Common Sense

You will begin to establish priorities and set boundaries. This will make your daily choices easier. Not only will the choices be easier, but the decisions you make will support the goals you have set. Your life will begin to function in a more harmonious manner with less stress, less confusion and a definite sense of success and purpose. All this will affect your handling of money, your political beliefs, your spirituality and even your sexuality. Every dimension of your life will be affected.

All of this is just common sense. It is using all of your resources. It is not relying on anyone else to tell you what is right for you. Take charge of your life by using your innate COMMON SENSE

Do not allow complacency to settle in. Muster the strength within to stay focused and don't give up. I share with people all the time a phrase that I love: "I HATE TO LOSE!" Make this a part of your vocabulary and repeat it often. Share it and, pretty soon, you and those that know you will expect you to be a winner because you hate to lose!

The rest of this book will make you aware of areas in your life in which to STAND UP, apply COMMON SENSE and change your life. Read on and you will begin thinking of new ways to apply COMMON SENSE and how you too can STAND UP to make a difference in your life and in the lives of others.

Notes

Chapter 2

Starting Over

This chapter is a challenging one, in that it attempts to connect with a very broad demographic: people that are underemployed, unemployed, and those who are struggling to find their nitch or to discover what their purpose in life is. It is my opinion that whoever you are, you need some basic fundamentals to get out of the starting gate and STAND UP to the task of charting the rest of your life.

One of the ways to begin is to relate with someone that has achieved. In this regard, I want to build on the mention of Thomas Paine in the previous chapter. He was not an orator like Patrick Henry, nor was he a leader like George Washington. At age thirty-five, he was a failure when he immigrated to Boston at the urging of his friend, Ben Franklin. Yet, he has gone down in American history as a key player and celebrated in history books.

Stand Up or Bend Over

And, I might add, he gets more than an honorable mention. I like Paine as a point of reference in this chapter, because he came to the colonies to start over. He had failed at marriage, business and was a drunkard. Mr. Franklin believed in him and encouraged him to immigrate to Boston. Paine had experience as a printer and he was able to get a job in a print shop.

However, his strength was in writing. He created the little book, "Common Sense," which sold over half a million copies in the colonies. He was recognized as an insightful, thoughtful writer who seemed to have the ability to make common sense out of a lot of seemingly unrelated pieces of information. His words had the uncanny ability to resonate with the people of the colonies. He was so talented a writer that General George Washington recruited him into the colonial army. His mission was not to carry a gun, ride a horse or carry messages.

This failure of a man was valued so much as a writer, that General Washington engaged him to write about events, battles, personalities and behind-the-scenes activities to encourage the army and citizens back at home. What a wonderful and true story about a real person during a most difficult time in his life—and in the life of a young nation—as Paine STARTED OVER. Paine was our first war correspondent. How's that for redefining yourself and STARTING OVER!

You will need to employ all the resources at your disposal to achieve whatever level of success you aspire to. You may for the first time have to get fully acquainted with yourself. A self-assessment can be a good place to start. I challenge you to sit down and be gut-level honest with yourself. Think back over your life and list all the critical crossroads or decisions you have encountered to date in your life.

Starting Over

Go back as far as you can remember. I was able to remember back to age two-and-a-half, when my grandparents went to court and gained custody of me. Once you have made the list of events or decisions that you have experienced, next identify who made each one of these decisions. Was it you? This is critical for you to determine if you made them. Did you make them to satisfy someone else? Were the decisions other-directed, someone imposing their authority or power over you?

The object of this exercise is to determine, as best you can, just what you have been in control of in your life. Maybe you have been under the illusion that you are a control freak and now find out that you haven't been in control of anything. What a revelation! Maybe this will help you go with the flow and respect other people's input as you chart the rest of your life. Be serious about this, because it is important that you be honest with yourself and engage with other people on a most respectful and productive basis.

Another important dimension relates to the exercise discussed above. Connecting the dots of seemingly unrelated events in your life can provide eye-opening insights. If you are willing to do this and you are honest, you may see for the first time the cause and effect between events that you have hitherto been unaware of. Try to remember what events caused you to feel a sense of pride, or where you received accolades for a job well done. These were most likely times when you were using your natural, God-given gifts and talents. It was likely easy and caused you little stress. It may have energized you, rather than exhausted you. It is important to reflect, to learn and to begin to capture the energy of those moments to help you move forward now. This is effectively equipping you from within. Make this reflection a permanent part of your daily routine. You will be able to reach farther, run faster and jump higher.

Stand Up or Bend Over

Living in the twenty-first century, in the Information Age, we are bewildered by all the options and choices. You have more tools and resources available than anyone in times past. Opportunities to apply your skills, training, natural gifts, experience and energy are unlimited. It's almost too much of a good thing. Confusion and distraction will reign if you can't focus and remain determined about what you will do for the rest of your life.

As you analyze your situation, your resources and the options you might choose from keep your attitude positive and attention focused. Yet this is difficult when nothing seems to be working and you are continually receiving negative responses. I'm reminded of Thomas Edison when he was developing the light bulb filament. When asked about his invention, he stated, "I speak without exaggeration when I say that I have constructed 3,000 different theories in connection with the electric light, each one of them reasonable and apparently likely to be true. Yet only in two cases did my experiments prove my theory."* Now that's a POSITIVE MENTAL ATTITUDE AND THE WILLINGNESS TO PERSEVERE!

Another important perspective to keep in mind is this. Very few people are good at all things. People that have demonstrated a capacity for making money are not necessarily good at managing money. The few wealthy people I have had the privilege of knowing were smart enough to engage someone else to manage their money. This even includes having someone set the boundaries or guidelines for their spending, saving and investing. Many people who have had a great idea for a business have failed for lack of planning, lack of managing skills or being under-funded. Seek out and surround yourself with the skills necessary to be successful

*Thomas Edison quote referenced from:
"*American Legends: The Life of Thomas Edison*" by Charles River Editors..

Starting Over

Read books that will provide you sound advice. You never know when some little nugget of information will be just the thing to help you connect the dots and turn fuzzy thoughts into a crisp, clear direction.

I want to share a personal story of an extreme starting over that has left a permanent mark in my memory. My wife and I had occasion to take a trip to Europe in 1985. One stop on that trip was a refugee camp in St. Nicole, Austria. The camp was sponsored by the United Nations and held approximately 2,000 refugees from behind the Iron Curtain. We had the opportunity to meet some of the people and to get to know them a bit. One couple had two small children, one of which had been born in the camp. They were very hospitable and shared their experience of leaving their homeland. At the time we met, they had already spent an entire year in the small one-room apartment assigned to them. After listening to their story, I asked them a question. Now, it is important to know that these people were educated and once had good jobs. The woman spoke good English and the man, somewhat.

I said to them, "You left your homeland and can't go back. You gave up your family, friends and all your possessions that wouldn't fit inside your two suitcases. You have been here an entire year and you do not know when you will leave. You also do not know where you will go. Why did you decide to do this?" The husband, who spoke broken English, quickly said, "I tell, I tell!"

He proceeded to say that they had an apartment and a television because they belonged to the Communist Party. They had jobs because they belonged to the Party. There was one channel on the TV, and it was the government channel telling them only what the government wanted them to know.

Stand Up or Bend Over

He would get up every morning and stand in line for one hour to get food for his family. Why did we leave? FOR FREEDOM! I truly felt like the stupid American. The family ultimately found a new home in Canada.

Their story has never left me. It has made me more grateful for living in the United States of America. It has made me aware of the plight of other not-so-fortunate people around the world. I tell the story here because it is an incredible story of STARTING OVER.   It is a story I believe every American should hear. Maybe, just maybe it will make Americans more aware of their blessings and their freedom. Maybe we will begin to understand why other people are rioting and rebelling against oppression and intolerant government regimes.

If you are facing the frightening situation of STARTING OVER, ponder giving up almost everything, like the refugees in the camp did, for freedom. What are you willing to give up for your freedom for the rest of your life?

Think about the challenges and circumstances so many people in America have met and, not just survived, but actually used as a springboard to launch themselves to new levels of achievement, joy and living.

Starting Over

Some pearls of wisdom:

*Lean not on thine own understanding.
Trust the Lord in all things.*

(Proverbs 3:5)

*Of myself I can do nothing.
With the Lord all things are possible.*

(Matthew 19:26)

As a man thinks, so is he.

(Proverbs 23:7)

Notes

Chapter 3

Fear

It is necessary to discuss fear in this book because it is one of the basic human emotions. It is often used effectively to control individuals or entire groups of people. Individually, we may be controlled by fear when we are faced with a new situation or circumstance. Fear of failure or embarrassment is shared by most people. Speaking in public is one of the top ten causes of fear.

When it comes to our personal finances, we may be fearful of exposure to others of the facts of our personal situation. Success, often measured by the apparent accumulation of money, has become extremely important in our society. People are more willing to discuss their sex life than the facts of their personal finances. This is indeed tragic, since so many people have no fundamental knowledge regarding money management, budgeting, goal-setting or investing. Maybe it is the fear of the lack of money management skills being exposed that causes people to avoid the money discussion.

Stand UP or Bend Over

Fear of not being approved for a loan. Fear of not being accepted at a particular college. Fear of rejection by someone. Fear manifests in different ways and will have different consequences. I believe it is vital to become determined to master fear and to not allow it to control you, your choices, your actions or your level of success. And it is my opinion that knowledge is the best weapon to fight fear. When you equip yourself with knowledge, you are not only empowered, but you also become fearless. Maybe it would be more appropriate to say you are more confident. Whichever it is, you will benefit by it and be able to live a less stressful and more fulfilling life.

Some examples of where fear affects our daily lives with respect to money are collection calls, rejection of credit applications, loss of income and paying bills. These are very real issues and can cause many sleepless nights. The financial world has been very creative in helping people avoid fear by creating all sorts of techniques to help us avoid it. I call these the "FEAR-DRIVEN STRATEGIES" of the credit world. Credit cards, debit cards and overdraft protection are three such techniques offered by the credit grantors. They actually can help you, but more often they are revenue-generating techniques promoted by the banks and credit card companies. We readily accept them to avoid experiencing fear and achieving better financial discipline.

Let's take a big fear that most people never thought they would face–defaulting on your home mortgage. This is the unthinkable event that too many people have faced recently. Fear sets in because your home is your safe zone. It is where you lay your head down at night, where you know you and your family are okay. When faced with mortgage default, fear comes in big time. Many questions begin to manifest. What will the mortgage company do? How long do I have before they throw me out? And every knock on the door or ring of the phone causes your heart to skip a beat.

Fear

"What can I do?" you ask.

Fear of the collectors.

Fear of the courts.

Fear of damaging your credit.

Fear of defaulting on your mortgage.

Fear of _____. You fill in the blank.

I now suggest to you that your fears are all based on a lack of knowledge about any number of these areas. Myths, misconceptions and half-truths are what comprise most people's knowledge in these areas that create fear. Credit scores are so important that people make decisions based on what will happen to their credit scores, yet they don't have a clue what they are really doing or how their decisions are impacting their credit scores!

Here's a case in point. A gentleman came in and asked if we could fix his credit. I said I didn't know, because I didn't know what was wrong with it. He proceeded to tell me he had charged $5,000 to $6,000 each month and paid in full every month before the due date. He said his credit scores were low and did not understand. I told him he could fix his credit scores very easily. FACT: The only thing that builds credit is making payments. Since he was paying his balances in full each month, the credit bureaus did not know he had charged anything or that he even paid a dime.

Stand Up or Bend Over

The creditors report monthly, and he was being reported every month with a zero balance which did not display any activity. It was as if he didn't even use his credit cards. I instructed him to leave a balance on each card each month and his credit score would rise to a very satisfactory level in a short time. HE DID! And IT DID!

For better or for worse, we live and die by our credit scores. But do you know what really affects your scores? How you can improve your scores? And how long it takes to recover from bankruptcy, foreclosure or repossession of a vehicle?

Continue reading the next chapter to learn more, including why you should not be afraid of what might happen to your credit score.

Notes

Notes

Chapter 4

Credit

Credit is one of the mysteries of our society. We are a credit-driven society. People live and die by their credit scores. With the high level of importance it has in our lives, strangely it is much like the Wizard from "The Wizard of Oz." Nobody gets to see the Wizard. The credit bureaus, along with Fair Isaac, guard this like the proverbial gold in Fort Knox. The software and formulas were all developed by Fair Isaac Corporation in Minneapolis, Minnesota. No one but Fair Isaac knows the formulas and how exactly they are weighted by a myriad of factors. Just like in "The Wizard of Oz," only the Wizard knows!

The three credit bureaus use these formulas, and yet you are left wondering why these three bureaus generate three different Fair Isaac scores. Some of the reason is that the databases are not identical for the three bureaus. Not all creditors report to all three bureaus. And each bureau has the ability to make mistakes unique to their database.

Stand Up or Bend Over

Not all court reporting systems are as prompt or as accurate as they should be in reporting judgments, liens or the releases of the same. There are people involved in the process, so you have the human factor contributing to the accuracy or inaccuracy as well. Therefore, different scores are generated, almost as if you were three different people.

The bureaus will tell you the possible range of scores, and some of the factors that affect your score, such as inquiries, debt ratio, late payments, liens, collection accounts, bankruptcy and foreclosure. Frankly, for the most part these items are fear factors to keep you in line and to keep you guessing. The information ultimately disseminated is not very revealing and not very helpful to the consumer. Hopefully, the information presented here will enable you to make wiser, more informed decisions relative to your credit. Please understand that I do not think like The Wizard, and I am not all-knowing! I am sharing with you what I have observed and learned over thirty years, helping people understand these critical factors in their lives.

We are so conscious of protecting our credit that the personal decisions and choices we make are pre-empted by the question, "What will it do to my credit?" Our choices are not always in our best interest and are often driven by what we think the impact will be. Unfortunately, decisions are frequently based on myths, half-truths and just plain false information.
Many people live in false fear of damaging their credit. They also live in false fear that, once damaged, it will take forever for their credit to recover.

It is my opinion that this is shrouded in mystery by design and on purpose. As personal as credit scores are, the process of analyzing and granting credit has become very impersonal. Most often in today's credit world, the decision to, or not to, grant credit is determined by a computer program designed by the credit issuer..

Credit

It is supposed to be idiot-proof and to treat all applications equally. What this means is that people processing the credit reports and reading the scores have virtually no authority or option to make a decision. It is done by "the system." When you are approved, you don't really know why. When you are denied, you are only told in broad terms why you were denied and are only told which credit bureau's information was used to make the determination. No one can help you, and no one is empowered to make a decision or override the system. Credit issuers spend a lot of money trying to convince you that they care and want to protect you. The truth is, they really don't care and are protecting themselves. They just want to convince you to use their services and their money. Nothing personal, just business! Most of the correspondence you receive pertaining to the rules of credit–changes to the agreement, how fees are applied, privacy policies, etc.–is not supplied out of the gracious concern of the creditor, but merely to keep the creditor in compliance with applicable laws.

Identity theft has been touted as the fastest growing crime in the United States. This has spawned the new business of ID Theft protection or credit insurance. And it is based on FEAR. Here is an important fact to remember: Three out of every four incidents of identity theft are perpetrated by a family member. I can attest to this personally by incidents we have seen in our office. Common sense and not being careless will certainly help protect you. My contention is that the professional thieves will get you no matter what you do. I do not make light of this problem. It is serious one. I just want you to know the facts and I also encourage you to be prudent. Hackers will breach computer firewalls to access data files and there just isn't much you can do about it. But please don't live in fear of what might happen. Do buy credit insurance if you feel you need it.

Stand Up or Bend Over

FACT: Bankruptcy and foreclosure will damage your credit. Yes, they will be appearing on your credit reports for ten years in the "public record" section of your credit report. The line items for the individual creditors will be on the report for seven years. These stipulations are per the Fair Credit Reporting Act (FCRA). It is necessary and appropriate for you to be proactive after either of these events have occurred. You should request your own credit report and examine it, or engage someone to examine your report to determine that everything is reporting correctly. We do not live in a perfect world and you should verify any report's accuracy.

POST BANKRUPTCY: Here I recommend you do two things. The first step, as suggested in the above paragraph, is to validate all three credit bureaus to verify that the information recorded—as a result of the bankruptcy—is correct. The second step is to be proactive to re-establish your credit. If you do nothing, the naysayers will be correct and your credit will be in the dumper for seven to ten years.

RE-ESTABLISHING CREDIT: What you can do to boost your scores:

1.) Get a credit card with a low credit limit. Spend only up to half of the credit limit. Then make small monthly payments to create a positive credit history.

2.) A secured card is a good choice if you need to repair a damaged credit history and can't get approved for a regular credit card. Secured credit cards will require a refundable security deposit to establish your credit line. This can be anywhere from $250 to $5,000. Keeping your secured credit card payments current helps to build a positive credit history, which may be shared with all three major credit bureaus.

STAND UP and take charge of your credit. The two steps recommended above will work miracles for you. Following the recommended process, some of our clients have qualified to buy another house at current market rates in only two-and-a-half years out of bankruptcy or foreclosure.

Credit

Remember, the negative items do stay on your reports for the required time periods. However, make certain they are neutralized by proper reporting and be aware that they have less impact as they move farther down the timeline. Your scores will improve quite nicely and you need not lose any sleep over them.

There are people out in the marketplace that promise the moon, the sun and the stars, with respect to removing items from your credit and making your credit perfect. Yet, oftentimes what they promise is illegal per the FCRA. Do not believe them. Do not pay them. You can do it yourself. Or, there are some good guys out there, you just need to find them.

The following facts will provide better insight for you to learn how your credit scores are affected by factual information that is supplied by your creditors.

Facts:

1. FCRA: All credit reporting by all three bureaus is regulated by the FAIR CREDIT REPORTING ACT (FCRA). This is a federal law and I recommend you become familiar with it–to know what is legal, what you can expect to change, and what you can't. It clarifies what the reporting time limits are for various pieces of information such as judgments, liens, collection accounts and late payments. It will be much easier to STAND UP if you do your homework. Visit the U.S. Federal Trade Commission's website at www.ftc.gov for more information.

2. Paying off your credit cards every month will not build credit. The only thing that builds credit is making payments and leaving a balance, even if only a small one. Leave a small balance on the account every month. Yes, it will cost some interest, but that is the price of building good credit.

Stand Up or Bend Over

3. Open ZERO-BALANCE, revolving credit accounts and credit cards will lower your scores if you have too many of them. We had a client come to us with sixteen open zero-balance accounts who wondered why her credit scores were so bad. Upon having her close thirteen of them, her scores immediately made a substantial rise.

4. If you have a DISPUTE with a creditor who is reporting incorrectly with the bureaus, you can send a written dispute to those bureaus and they must contact the creditor. The creditor has thirty days to respond to the bureau. If they do not respond in thirty days, the bureau must remove it from your report. If they do respond, the bureau must respond to what they say and notify you of the result. This is a good technique to make certain that collection agencies report accurately and that errors are corrected. Remember, if the creditor or collection agency does not respond in thirty days to the credit bureau, the item must be deleted from your credit report.

5. MAXED-OUT CREDIT CARDS: When credit card balances rise above fifty percent of the card limit, your scores go down. Keep the balance to less than half of the limit. You can then spread the balances over all your cards to maximize your scores.

6. COLLECTION ACCOUNTS: Often when a collection account is pulled from one collection agency and assigned to another, the previous agency does not remove it. This puts you in double jeopardy. Oftentimes when an agency has several accounts with one client, they report only one or two of them. This happens frequently with medical accounts. You can be certain that when you respond to the agency, they will advise you of the other accounts. If you are negatively affected by erroneous information or non-reporting of information, you may also be entitled to damages. Check with a consumer affairs attorney in such cases.

Credit

7. LATE PAYMENTS: Your contract with a creditor will stipulate when payments are due and when they are late. Normally, they will assess a late fee some number of days after the due date. This does not mean that your account will be reported to the credit bureau as a late payment merely because you were assessed a late fee. Credit reporting purposes normally deem an account late only when it is thirty-one days past the due date. Creditors normally report monthly to the bureaus, so it is not a real-time system. You need not worry about your credit until you are over thirty-one days late on the payment.

8. CREDIT SCORES: The credit scores you pay for when you request a free credit report may be different than the scores reported to a creditor. I recently read in the Wall Street Journal that there are no less than 49 versions of your FICO score made available to lenders. I can only imagine these variations are based on factors they won't tell you about.

9. USE OF CREDIT SCORES: Credit scores are being used for ever-increasing intrusions into our lives. Nobody asks us how such personal information about us should be used. Credit approval, health and auto insurance rating for determining premiums, job application reviews, receipts of unsolicited invitations to apply for pre-approved credit cards, and the tracking of shopping habits are a few examples. And I am certain there are more we don't know about.

Truth vs. Myth

The following is an example of the credit impact from defaulting on credit cards, negotiating the balances and then being proactive restoring one's credit.

Situation: A couple with a home mortgage, over $80,000 of credit card debt and negative monthly cash flow; home mortgage interest rate at 5.25% and credit cards all above 20% interest. The couple secured a new cash-out mortgage loan to provide money to negotiate their credit card debt. Because of their debt ratio, they had to pay a premium mortgage rate on the new loan of 9.5%.

In eight months, start to finish, the credit cards were negotiated at a savings of approximately $40,000. The credit scores were rebuilt to higher scores. A new mortgage was secured eight months after they started the process and–due to a reduced debt ratio and improved credit scores–the new mortgage interest rate was now 5.5%. They also ended up with a positive cash flow in excess of $1,200 per month, with the principle on the old credit card debt rolled into the new mortgage at a lower rate! And it was tax deductible. This particular client STOOD UP and won.

Positive monthly cash flow, monthly savings, improved credit–all accomplished in eight months. They could sleep soundly. Stress was reduced and no more discussions about who gets paid this month. No escalated arguments caused by financial distress.

Credit

Miracles Do Happen

The following is another factual case from several years ago. A new client came to me and asked if we negotiated credit cards. I assured him we did. He said he had five credit cards, all with the same creditor.

The total was approximately $55,000 and the accounts were all current. The client had lost his job and wanted to get the debt off his back. He felt able to do this, as he had received a separation payment from his employer and it was large enough to wipe out the debt if we could make a deal. I told him it would take some time, as he would have to default on the payments– to position the creditor to be willing to negotiate. He agreed and decided to have us proceed..

Normally I would wait for sixty to ninety days to contact the creditor. However, for some reason I contacted the creditor immediately to give them a heads up. I advised them that my client had lost his job and the five accounts would be going delinquent, and that we would follow up in sixty to ninety days.

Now this is where the story gets interesting. The person on the phone asked what we wanted to do. I explained the situation in more detail and stated we were looking for a settlement. The person asked how much we were expecting. When I told her, she said it would take a day or two, but she would call me back .

Stand Up or Bend Over

I received a call within twenty-four hours and was shocked when the representative told me the settlement had been approved! I didn't ask any questions. Rather, I asked that a letter be faxed stating the terms of the settlement. That was promptly done and my client was able to pay the agreed settlement.

After leting the dust settle for a couple of days, I called the representative back. I explained that she had blown me away with her very quick and affirmative response, and that I was calling to find out exactly what I had done right to succeed. She proceeded to enlighten me. And I almost fainted.

She said she checked the record and found that my client had these cards for a long time. He had maintained a substantial balance for a long time. He had a good payment history for a long time. She also told me they know that bad things happen to good people. As a result of the history and the facts, they would be willing to help my client in this troubled time and looked to get him back as a customer in the future. HOW REFRESHING AND PRACTICAL!

I never had this happen before and never has it happened again. It was the most rational, logical and most common sense approach to solving a problem I have encountered in many years. And though it happened only once, it could also happen for you if you STAND UP and try. My client's credit didn't even take a hit.

Why can't more creditors be like this?

Credit

Don't Charge! Take Charge!

The 3 national credit bureaus that hold all the credit information are;

Equifax
P.O. Box 740241
Atlanta, GA 30374
1-800-685-1111
www.equifax.com/fcra

Trans Union
P.O. Box 2000
Chester, PA 19022-2000
1-800-888-4213
www.transunion.com

Experian
P.O. Box 2104
Allen, TX 75013
1-888-397-3742
www.experian.com/reportaccess

I strongly recommend you communicate with the bureaus in writing rather than calling. It provides proof and, hopefully, communicates clearly what needs to be done. It is more efficient and less frustrating than waiting on the phone. My experience is that they do respond in writing to written requests, which makes things easier in our busy world. It also provides hard copies for future reference.

Stand Up or Bend Over

IF YOU ARE GOING TO PLAY THE GAME, YOU NEED TO KNOW THE RULES.

Your credit score is important and you need to make sound decisions to optimize it. Do not operate in fear or ignorance. Do not let these things control you or your decisions. Empower yourself with knowledge! Make your decisions based on what is in your best interest. And definitely do not let your decisions result in the benefit of the creditor.

FOR YOUR PROTECTION – THINGS YOU NEED TO KNOW

Go online and check out the following when you encounter problems. These resources are available for your protection, but they won't help you if you are ignorant about how to apply the law to your situation or circumstances. Both of these are federal laws and apply across the country.

FAIR CREDIT REPORTING ACT (FCRA) This act sets the rules for reporting your credit information. It stipulates how long it is reported, along with procedures for administration and correction of misinformation. THINGS YOU NEED TO KNOW! Visit the U.S. Federal Trade Commission website at www.ftc.gov for more information.

Credit

FAIR DEBT COLLECTION PRACTICES ACT
(FDCPA) This act governs the practices of the creditor and any third party collector or purchaser of old debts. It sets the rules and outlines the penalties for when the rules are violated. You should be familiar with this information to protect yourself from unscrupulous collection actions–who they can call, when they can call, what they can say. YOU NEED TO KNOW! Visit the U.S. Federal Trade Commission website at www.ftc.gov for more information.

STATUTE of LIMITATIONS
Every state has a statute of limitations that regulates how old an account can be while remaining legally enforceable. This means that for a collector to collect a debt, an attorney is sometimes hired to secure a judgment against you to have a garnishment attached to your wages or a lien placed on your property. Such time limits vary by state. Statutes may also vary for secured debts, depending on the security. The latest information I have is that limits range from 3 to 10 years, depending on the state and the type of debt. If you have any questions about your personal situation, you should check the laws in your state. In fact, YOU NEED TO KNOW!!

If you are finding this information helpful, please visit our website for other resources including online classes, books, webinars and more at: **www.standuporbendover.net**

The Choice Is Yours

Notes

Chapter 5

Consumer Protection

The topic of consumer protection is a strange one. Legislative bodies all over the country, especially the U.S. Congress, seem bent on protecting the consumer. I believe their intent is admirable and I am not suggesting we shouldn't have consumer protections. The Food and Drug Administration (FDA), the Environmental Protection Agency (EPA), and the host of other financial, health, public safety and animal control regulations administered by attorney generals and other agencies are good in principle.

Much legislation has been created as a knee-jerk reaction to combat unscrupulous business practices discovered after the fact, and they are hastily enacted. Part of my concern is that with such a plethora of laws to protect consumers, most remain unknown to the consumer.

Stand Up or Bend Over

When laws are enacted, the consumer often doesn't know how he has been protected, or how to even determine if he has been violated. Even when an enforcement agency determines a violation has occurred, the net effect on the consumer is virtually nothing. Evidence of this includes homeowners across the country that have been wrongfully foreclosed on, after gross violations of the laws have been proven. And what does the consumer get? THE SHAFT!

If the government wants to protect the consumer, why not begin in the critical area of prevention, rather than after the fact? The poor consumer who has already been had gets nothing. How much does a consumer get when a class action suit is settled? How much money will the injured mortgagors of Bank of America get from the $27,000,000,000 settlement? The finite wisdom of the legislatures is usually in looking back, and not in anticipation of what is going to happen in the future.

As much as I try not to be cynical, sometimes I just can't help myself. The legislative process at the state and federal levels has become a tool of special interest groups, and the consumer is left out of the equation entirely (except in name). All the specialist interest groups, lobbyists and politicians trying to make a name for themselves set out to pass legislation that has a great sounding name, wrapped in the guise of CONSUMER PROTECTION. The net effect is off the mark, because the legislation is written in such a broad scope that both the good guys and the bad guys are knocked out of the game. The inability of the legislatures to write laws that allow the good guys to continue operating and the authorities to distinguish the difference between the rascals and the saints seems next to impossible.

Consumer Protection

The very concept implies that legislatures would have to clearly understand the workings of the marketplace and deceptive advertising, and to rely on factual feedback from educated consumers. It would also mean that there would have to exist fair and equitable enforcement when violations are proven and that consumers are compensated in such cases.

I believe the consumer within the current system is actually hurt, since the good guys are wiped out alongside the bad guys. The consumer is left to paddle for himself.

A current example: The energy-efficient products replacing the old incandescent light bulbs—proudly produced in America by Americans—were outlawed. The January 2012 deadline for ending sale of the old incandescent bulbs was rescinded. I suspect this is a good case for a study in "follow the money." The president of GE is politically connected in Washington D.C. During this time, GE closed their American facility and shipped the manufacturing offshore. The new energy-efficient bulbs are now actually deemed harmful! All in the name of consumer protection and energy conservation. Oh yes, the new bulbs are so dangerous that, if broken, you now need a special clean up crew to keep you from being contaminated. This is not consumer protection. I also recently heard that energy-efficient bulbs can be harmful if we are too close to them while they are on.

GOVERNMENT, GET OUT OF MY FACE!

Stand Up or Bend Over

Predator Creditors

It is important to know that a clause exists embedded in Payday Loans. Which when you sign for a Payday Loan, the creditor has the authority to garnish your wages without going to court for a judgment. This is not a desirable for you to approve in advance. And they can keep taking your money long after the principal is paid off. Where is the consumer protection?

Title loans are a bit more obvious in that you give up the title to your vehicle as collateral for the loan you are granted. If you don't pay, they have the legal right to take your car.

It is not unusual to see 200% to over 500% interest charged on these types of loans. Unfortunately, this is legal. So be wise. Be careful. Avoid such options, as they are a financial straight jacket. They will only lead to deeper depression, higher anxiety and greater fear.

These are only extreme options to which consumers turn out of desperation, frustration or other emotional responses, only to get caught in a trap that quickly goes from bad to worse. When you find yourself considering such options as the solution to your problem, STOP. Take a deep breath, swallow your pride and rethink your situation and your options.

There are few usury laws to protect you. And remember that desperate people do desperate things. Knowledge, common sense and reality must prevail.

Consumer Protection

Mortgages

The last decade has proven, on a grand scale, the ineptness and immorality of the mortgage industry. The mortgage industry, Wall Street, and the Government hoodwinked the authorities, regulators, examiners and czars to make it appear they were "helping every American to achieve the American dream." These are the words our representatives used in Congress to defend the unscrupulous practices of the mortgage companies, Wall Street and the government agencies of Fannie Mae and Freddie Mac.

Now come the knee-jerk reactions by the very people that should have been providing the CONSUMER PROTECTION. Of course, all we get are excuses coupled with smoke and mirrors from Washington. Oh yes, we've seen some actions taken both by states and by the feds to sue the mortgage companies, actually achieving some favorable decisions. At least, it would seem so.

Bank of America was sued by the feds and eighteen states. An agreement was reached by the plaintiffs and Bank of America. Now we need to examine results. What will be achieved with the $27 billion settlement awarded eighteen states and the feds from Bank of America and others? It will not give any relief to homeowners that were fraudulently induced to sign mortgage documents which are still being enforced by the court system (which said Bank of America broke the law). I understand that $2 billion was allocated to the State of Illinois for Bank of America mortgagors. How much will trickle down to the victimized homeowner with a mortgage held by Bank of America?

Stand Up or Bend Over

The sad part is that, to my knowledge, no amount for the individual homeowner has been announced and, even when it is, the poor homeowner will still be saddled with the original mortgage that will not have changed. The homeowner will still have the same high interest rate and, in too many cases, negative equity, because there was no provision to adjust the mortgage balance to the market value. Restructure of loans has been announced by some mortgage companies, but so far it seems to be only lip service.

The winners are the attorneys that received their fees and the politicians that claim they won a victory for their constituency. It will sound good in the next campaign for re-election. The homeowner will still lose his house or continue to make fraudulently induced payments if he can afford it. Even if the homeowner receives $1,000, it's like spitting in the ocean.

In 2008, Illinois passed another piece of legislation that put the mortgage brokers out of business. I am sure there were some bad brokers. The legislation was purportedly passed to protect consumers from unscrupulous BAD GUYS who were cheating consumers.

However, there were some very reputable service providers who were also swept out of business with the new broom of integrity and protection, propelled by the legislature that didn't understand what it was doing because it couldn't distinguish between the good guys and the bad guys. Brokers do provide a valuable service to consumers.

No one ever said that being a legislator would be easy. However, it carries with it the need to be discerning, wise and fair, and to remember you are accountable to the electorate, not the lobbyist.

Price Fixing

Whatever happened to price fixing laws? Why do government regulators and enforcers ignore the ever-changing gasoline prices (mostly upward) that all change in unison like the voices in a choir?

And while we're on the topic of gasoline…Examination of a British Petroleum (BP) financial report showed a profit of $.06 per gallon, which spawned a discussion with a friend who felt this was an excessive amount for what he considers a terrible petro company. After all, $.06 per gallon for all the gallons of gasoline BP sells is a staggering number. Let's do a comparison just for kicks. The total tax paid by the consumer on a gallon of gas ranges from $.40 to $.60, depending on the state. This includes all federal, state and local taxes levied by each jurisdiction.

Would it not be appropriate to ask the question: Why are the combined government bodies entitled to 6 to 10 times the income on a gallon of gasoline, when sold by a petroleum company which bears all the risk, investment and expense of bringing the product to market? The only risk incurred by the government is re-election!

Actually, the total tax per gallon is something greater than the tax at the pump, since oil companies have already paid corporate tax, payroll tax, property tax, business tax and more. This is not consumer protection. BEND OVER at the pump!

Stand Up or Bend Over

Do You Know?

The legal profession is very specialized. Just as the medical profession has specialists like podiatrists, eye ear nose & throat doctors, dermatologists, surgeons, etc., the legal profession has bankruptcy, foreclosure, divorce, corporate, patent and CONSUMER PROTECTION ATTORNEYS. These folks are largely unheralded champions of the people. Now remember, I am not an attorney and I cannot speak for all of them. However, my experience with them has been very good, so I recommend you listen closely to the material presented in this section.

The first challenge to you is to discover when your rights may have been violated. As I have already mentioned, there are many laws on the books to protect the consumer. And you, the consumer, usually don't have a clue. You need to be aware and know where to go if you think you may have been violated. You also need to know how and where to find a consumer protection or consumer affairs attorney. I will answer the second question first.

I urge you to contact your local or state bar to find out who practices consumer protection in your jurisdiction. I recommend this approach over the yellow pages or the internet.

Now, to address the first question as to how to discover, or even have reason to suspect, you have been violated. I want to thank my friend and professional resource, Dan Edelman, a partner in a consumer protection law firm in Chicago, with whom I have had the pleasure of working. He has here provided the following material to help create awareness of the broad scope of consumer protection laws that may be beneficial to you.

Consumer Protection

Ways You Are Protected!

TIME BARRED DEBTS: Something beyond the statute of limitation.

DEBT COLLECTOR PHONE MESSAGES: The messages left on your voice mail or answering machine may be violations. You might want to save them and call a consumer affairs attorney.

CALLS FROM A DEBT COLLECTOR TO YOUR EMPLOYER, RELATIVES, FRIENDS OR NEIGHBORS: Is a debt collector calling people other than you to collect a debt from you?

BALANCE TRANSFER OFFERS: It may not be prudent to accept the offer and the offer could violate the law.

GRAVEYARD COLLECTIONS: Are debt collectors calling or writing you to collect the debt of a deceased family member?

NURSING HOME COLLECTIONS: Is your elderly parent or spouse in a nursing home? Is the nursing home trying to collect the costs of the stay from you?

HIGH INTEREST LOAN COLLECTIONS: Are collectors trying to collect illegal high-interest loans made over the internet? Most such loans are illegal.

JUNK FAXES: Have you received one or more spam faxes from companies with whom you have never had any prior dealings? You could potentially recover $1,500 for each unsolicited fax received under the Telephone Consumer Protection Act.

Stand Up or Bend Over

SPAM TEXT MESSAGES: Have you received spam texts on your cell phone from a company you have never had dealings with? You could potentially recover $1,500 for each such message.

FORCED PLACED INSURANCE: This is typically done by mortgage companies when they claim you have not paid your insurance.

CAR LOAN PAYOFF: Delay by dealer to pay off your trade-in when you purchased a vehicle.

CALLS TO CELL PHONES: If you did not provide the number, there may be a violation. Telemarketing and collection calls are covered.

UNAUTHORIZED CREDIT INQUIRIES: Inquiries you did not apply for or authorize.

SECURITY DEPOSIT VIOLATIONS: Refusing to pay you interest or failing to provide you your refund.

CREDIT & DEBIT CARD RECEIPTS: Does the receipt show more than the last five digits of your card number?

CREDIT CARD INSURANCE PLANS: Did you sign up for your credit card company's "payment protection plan" or similar insurance plan? Did your credit card company refuse to pay when you lost your job or became disabled?

FALSE INFORMATION ON YOUR CREDIT REPORT: Is there one or more false items on your credit report? Are you the victim of identity theft? Have the credit bureaus of Equifax, Transunion or Experian mixed up your information with that of somebody else? Have the creditors or bureaus refused to make corrections?

Consumer Protection

CREDIT INQUIRIES: Are you the authorized user (not the account holder) of a credit card? Did the credit card company or debt collector look at your credit file? Depending on the circumstances, it could be a violation of the law.

GIFT CARD EXPIRATION DATES: Is there an expiration date of less than five years?

WAGE CLAIMS: Does your employer make you work overtime and not pay you for it?

IINACCURATE BACKGROUND CHECKS: Was a background check done on you and confused with someone else with the same or a similar name?

This is not an exhaustive list of all possible consumer violations you might experience. However, this should give you insight into what to look for and be aware of, so you can STAND UP to the bad guys looking to take advantage of you.

Not every event is a violation. Trust your gut. If you have an uneasy feeling and believe that "if it smells, it's probably rotten," this would be a reasonable basis to check it out and seek the help of a professional.

What constitutes proof you are responsible for the debt?

When you receive a collection call you should not admit or agree with anything until they have provided proof of the debt and their right to collect it from you. A statement with your name on it is not proof that you owe the debt to the debt collector. Even if you know it is yours, don't admit or agree to anything. A signed agreement, contract or application, are the types of documentation that may prove you are responsible for the debt.

How long can a debt be legally enforced or collected?

The statute of limitations provides a time window (limit) within which a creditor can enforce collection of a debt. This varies by type of debt and the state that has jurisdiction. It generally varies from 3 to 10 years. You should check your state's laws to determine what applies to you and the situation you are facing.

There may be a violation of the law if you are called at work or on your cell phone, when you did not give the caller your number.

Consumer Protection

Things You Might Want to Consider

The following is a list of consumer protection laws that are applicable to consumer financing. The legislation has provided all the verbiage, intent, penalties and legalese embodied in the list of protections for you, the consumer. How many have you heard of? How many do you know something about? Do you know what the consequences are if they are violated? Do you know there is such a thing as a consumer affairs attorney? Have you ever attempted to learn your rights by familiarizing yourself with consumer protection laws?

We have heard that ignorance of the law is no excuse. We have also heard the phrase, "BUYER, BEWARE." But does this apply to the consumer who didn't know he was supposedly protected?

Laws Created to Protect You

This is not an exhaustive list, but an indication of the more prevalent and common statutes.

Real Estate Settlement Procedures Act	RESPA
FAIR Credit Reporting Act	FCRA
Truth in Landing Act	TILA
Mortgage Rescue Fraud Act (Illinois)	MRFA
Telephone Consumer Protection Act	TCPA
Fair Debt Collections Practices Act	FDCPA

These laws are all available to view on the internet. Educate yourself so you will be able to gain the protection you need when you need it. Of course, it takes time, effort and commitment to prepare yourself so you can benefit.

Stand Up or Bend Over

Agencies that Enforce Consumer Protection Laws

FDA (FOOD & DRUG ADMIN)
FDIC (FEDERAL DEPOSIT INSURANCE CORP)
ENVIRONMENTAL PROTECTION AGENCY (EPA)
ATTORNEY GENERAL of FEDERAL GOVERNMENT
STATES ATTORNEY GENERAL at the STATE LEVEL
STATE INSURANCE COMMISSION

Some state and federal agencies monitor compliance of professional groups like CPAs and investment advisors, and industries like financial institutions, hospitals, collection agencies and food service.

It behooves you to have some awareness of the potential for your rights to be violated and knowledge of who to turn to for help when you have reason to believe you've been had. Pay attention. Not everyone is as honest as you.

It's Up to You!

Notes

Notes

Chapter 6

How to Stand Up

Up to this point, I have tried to identify typical situations in which the consumer can be caught up in the emotion, lack of knowledge and frustration of everyday personal finances. I have also provided some information to arm you for the next encounter.

This book has pointed out the abuses and what is wrong. I have tried to encourage you to STAND UP and defend yourself with knowledge, strategies and the belief that you can do it. I have mustered the troops for you. Some people probably haven't read to this point. Well, that's their problem.

This is a call to the people of America to wake up! We have been lulled into a false sense of security and state of complacency.

It has all been reinforced with repeated statements from many corners–that business, politics and our world in general has become too complicated and too much to cope with. And if we really believe this, the show is over. PERIOD. END OF GAME!

Stand Up or Bend Over

Next I will provide some simple, factual, realistic strategies you can use to STAND UP. There is something here for everyone. These next pages contain practical ideas that can be applied by everyone. They are the meat and potatoes of the book, the part you have been waiting for. Where the rubber meets the road. Read on and decide which of the following you relate to, have a need for, or can begin to use today to STAND UP. If you don't get some traction from this chapter, you may need to check your pulse!

COLLECTION PHONE CALLS

Have you ever experienced those pesky and irritating phone calls that set you off because you don't know what to do? Maybe you've encountered creditors and collection companies that are relentless, intimidating, or just plain rude and arrogant. Well, you don't have to take it. STAND UP and fight back! The problem is most people don't know how to do this. Let me give you some basic instructions.

> **Don't** get mad.
> **Don't** lose your temper.
> **Don't** blow your cool.
> **Don't** defeat yourself.
> **GET EVEN!**

Get a name, note the time and take notes. Let them run off at the mouth with all the threats, foul language, arrogance and intimidation they are capable of. Then, as best you can, put it down verbatim.

How to Stand Up

Most often this will be enough to hang them, thanks to the Fair Debt Collection Practices Act (FDCPA), a federal law. Once you have collected the damning evidence, you have two choices:

You can seek out a consumer affairs attorney to take the case, or you can take your case to the management of the creditor. Most consumer advocate attorneys will review the case and take it on a contingency basis, if they determine your rights or any laws have been violated. This means you may get paid, and the attorney gets paid if they win the case for you. However, they get paid by the creditor or their agent who committed the violation, not by you. Depending on the severity of the violations, a debt may be erased or, in most cases, at least reduced. And you may also collect damages per the FDCPA. STAND UP!

You will feel good about yourself. You will probably reduce the number of creditors hounding you. And you may be richer in dollars, and in confidence, because you beat them at their own game. Educate yourself, know when the rules are broken, and be prepared to take action.

STAND UP ON THEIR TURF

STATUTE OF LIMITATIONS
– Knowledge is Power

"Friendly and kind" is one of the techniques used by collection companies on accounts that are old or may have aged beyond the statute of limitations. The creditor or collection company will call and actually offer to be kind to you.

Stand Up or Bend Over

They may tell you that the account is about to "go to legal" to get a judgment against you. However, if you will just make a minimal payment now, with a check by phone, they will keep the account from going to legal. This all sounds plausible and might seem to be an act of kindness on their part.

The fact is that the account is actually beyond the statute of limitation to enforce through the courts. If you respond to their kind offer and give them a payment as requested, you just reset the clock and the account is now enforceable in court. Don't take the bait!

You must know the rules of the game, or you lose. Rather than make the payment, you should demand that they send you proof of the debt and evidence that it is actually yours. Do not admit to or agree to anything until that is done.

STAND UP! WISE UP!

FIND THE DECISION MAKER
– Go to the Top

Don't have enough money to pay the bills?

Your credit cards have interest rates of 18% to 29%, and you can't make the minimum payments. You call them to explain your hardship and to ask for some relief. They tell you they don't have a program for you. Now is when you have to dig your heels in and push until you find the person in authority who is empowered to make a decision to really help you.

How to Stand Up

Depending upon the delinquency of the account, you may have to speak with various departments from collections, pre-legal, loss mitigation or the legal department. The ultimate contact might be the office of the president. That's right! Go all the way to the top. But don't expect to speak with the chief executive himself. However, be certain there's a staff of people ready to handle problems that escalate to this level. Be factual, honest, unemotional, pleasant (but firm) and determined. Ask them what they will do for you before you make any demands from them. And be reasonable. People at this level are professional, capable and empowered to solve problems, as well as to maintain good customer relations.

You can easily find addresses, phone numbers, fax numbers and email addresses on the internet.

STAND UP! ESCALATE THE PROBLEM!

CHALLENGE YOUR INSURANCE
Homeowners...Auto...Boat...Trailer...Toys

Review all your insurance policies each year when they are up for renewal. You may want to do some comparison shopping. By having my independent agent do the work, I recently saved $500 on my annual auto insurance, with no change in coverage or deductible. I also saved $2,000 last year on Medicare supplement insurance premiums merely by switching companies. Insurance companies have no loyalty to you, so why should you be loyal to them?

Stand Up or Bend Over

Homeowners insurance is very volatile and suspect at this time. Due to heavy losses and low return on their investments, some companies have ceased writing homeowner policies. Make certain any company has accurate specifications of your home. Size, construction, age, building materials, number of baths, finished basement and more are required to accurately determine the proper premium.

Contact your insurance agent to do the research for you, if he or she is an independent agent. If you are insured with a company that is exclusive with your agent, you may want to seek out an independent agent for some comparison shopping. This should be an annual event when your policy comes up for renewal.

It is not just a one-time savings. It should be for this year, the next year and so on.

STAND UP, GET THE IDEA?

BUYING A CAR - Do Your Homework

If you are going to purchase a vehicle, you would be wise to do your homework and make the necessary moves to be pre-approved for a vehicle loan before you walk into the dealership. Shop around. Go to your bank or credit union to apply for a loan and get pre-approved. This will help you make a more rational decision and, hopefully, keep the emotion out of the deal. Separate the financial part of the deal from the emotional part of touching, seeing and visualizing yourself in that driver's seat while you are in the showroom. You have then overcome a huge pitfall of overextending yourself. The wrong approach may put you into a financial straight jacket for a long time.

How to Stand Up

When you walk into a dealership, let them know you are going to buy a vehicle and you are pre-approved. You have just taken control from the salesman and the finance person. They must meet your terms. You know what price you can pay and you have strengthened your position in dealing with the dealer. There will be no hassle with their finance and insurance person (the F&I Manager), because you will have done your homework. You won't spend more than you can afford, and the monthly payment will not break your budget. These are all determined in the pre-approval process.

STAND UP! TAKE CONTROL!

RETAIL DISCOUNT

Sometimes the opportunity to stand up is hidden from you. I was recently made aware that The Home Depot and Lowes have a policy of giving 10% discounts on all purchases to all active, retired or honorably discharged veterans and their immediate family. You only must provide proper ID as proof of service. This is not usually advertised, you have to ask for it. If you don't ask, you don't get it!

Thanks to The Home Depot and Lowes!

STAND UP! ASK!

RELATIONSHIPS

I have referenced the fact that credit is very impersonal. Now that you know how the credit system works from behind the scenes, you can be proactive and do something to help yourself before the next crisis arises.

Stand Up or Bend Over

Our age of ATMs, direct deposits, drive-up windows, online banking and automated payments puts a lot of distance between you and your banker. This all contributes to a very impersonal relationship.

A way to help yourself is to be personable, rather than impersonal, in your relationships with the businesses you do business with. Let's take your bank as an example.

Drive-up windows are convenient and efficient. Yet they are very impersonal. Whenever you can, get out of your vehicle, STAND UP and walk into the bank. Make friends, so that when you walk in they address you by name. This will help you when you really need help from your banker. Someday you may need a loan or you may have a problem with your account, because of mistakes you or they made (it does happen).

It's is all about relationships. BUILD THEM!

STAND UP! DON'T DRIVE UP!

GET INVOLVED - Attend Meetings

Every government body that operates on a budget is funded with your tax dollars. They work for you. You pay them. And, in most cases, they, their budgets and actions are under the authority of the public servants you may have helped to elect. Your responsibility doesn't end with your vote for your preferred candidate. Attending meetings to learn how they are spending and managing your tax dollars is vital to the success of the system.

How to Stand Up

Unfortunately, most people don't attend these meetings and for a host of reasons. They are too busy. They don't understand how the meetings are conducted. Nobody will listen to them. Yet if you do not attend or participate–at least to listen and try to understand what is happening with your tax dollars–then you deserve whatever happens to your tax bill.

A recent school board town meeting to discuss a proposed referendum (more money) was attended by approximately one hundred tax payers. The result, after two meetings, was a decision by the board that the idea wasn't a good one. Therefore, there was no referendum and no additional taxes. If those people had not attended and participated, I can only imagine what would have happened! .

STAND UP AT THE MEETINGS

ADVERSITY INTO OPPORTUNITY
- You Can Do It!

Tough times call for knowledge. They also call for a plan of action.

The human spirit is very strong and resilient, especially in the face of adversity. And as you think, so are you. Don't defeat yourself with all the negative thoughts, trying to digest the news of the day. It's a downer and you don't need that sort of input. Be like the "Little Engine That Could." I think I can, I think I can, I think I can…and he did.

Without purpose, you lose. You may be facing foreclosure, bankruptcy or divorce and feel like your life is over. I challenge you to begin thinking the best is yet to come. You only need to get through the muck and mire of today.

Stand Up or Bend Over

It's time to STAND UP and take charge of your life. You must be determined to change your situation and your circumstances and move on. Setting goals gives you purpose and developing a plan gives you a roadmap to navigate through all the obstacles that jump out in front of you on the road of life.

Positive self-talk and surrounding yourself with positive people will do wonders in helping you stay positive and focused. Load yourself with depressed people, drugs and alcohol, and you lose!

STAND UP! BE DETERMINED

BANKRUPTCY

The very word instills terror and fear in most people. The main reasons are pride, fear of the unknown, the thought that your credit will be destroyed and that it will cost you a ton of money. Yet what you need to do is face reality, get educated and stop listening to the naysayers who spout nothing but bad stuff. Bankruptcy is referred to as "a fresh start." This is the only time I have ever known when the federal government will show mercy and give you some grace.

1. Educate yourself and begin to develop your plan.

2. Choose the time to file so that it fits in your timetable. Schedule it when it is to your advantage and in your best interest. Most attorneys will not counsel you on this aspect of bankruptcy.
   You will have to figure it out for yourself. You might want to visit www.minutemanfinancial.com and take the course on bankruptcy. It covers all the planning and timing necessary, along with the post-bankruptcy recovery of your credit.

How to Stand Up

3. Post-bankruptcy credit recovery is very important. Again, this is not an area your attorney will coach you with or advise you in. You need to verify that the bankruptcy is accurately represented on your credit reports, and then be proactive rebuilding your credit. Here, Minutemanfinancial.com might help you.

4. Use the internet to obtain forms, become educated and learn more about the bankruptcy process. For more information, visit: www.gov.com

I have had clients that filed for bankruptcy who, only two-and-a-half years after the discharge, were approved to buy another house at prime mortgage rates. Get additional help at: www.standuporbendover.net

STAND UP! START OVER!

FORECLOSURE

This is a potential trauma for almost everyone. Your home is your safe place to lay your head. All of a sudden, you find yourself in a situation along with twenty-five million other Americans. It shakes you to your very foundation, causing you to wring your hands and think, "What can we do?"

This is one of the most preeminent crises in America today. And you are not alone. The good news is there is help. And it is not from the government or the mortgage company. In most cases, the mortgage company will offer to do nothing that is in your best interest. You are the principle combatant, and you need to STAND UP! Do not expect the enemy to solve your problems.

Stand Up or Bend Over

FACT: I am not an attorney.
I CANNOT GIVE YOU LEGAL ADVICE.
You need to seek legal counsel.

In most cases, your mortgage company does not want your home. But you need to decide if you want to stay in the home. Some people don't want to stay, for whatever reason.

A good foreclosure defense attorney will be your best ally. His cost to you will be a less than if you go it alone in court against experienced foreclosure attorneys.

If you choose to stay in your home, then get legal counsel, STAND UP against the mortgage company and fight! The probability is high that you will win.

If you choose to not stay in your home, you will also be well advised to seek legal counsel. A lawyer can help you understand the process and when it is in your best interest to leave. Remember, attorneys are like doctors. They specialize, and they don't all know everything. In this case, you will need a foreclosure defense attorney. Contact your local legal Bar Association.

Either way, you need to STAND UP. Stand your ground and take control of your situation. You may actually be facing an opportunity of a lifetime. People all over the country are still in their homes after one or two years (or longer) of not making mortgage payments. Don't give up until you have to, until **you** choose to no longer occupy the house.

Additional help finding legal counsel is available at: **www. standuporbendover.net**
STAND UP! STAY IN YOUR HOME!

How to Stand Up

DIVORCE

This is, for many, one of life's greatest tragedies. Too often it breaks the heart, bends the mind, and sends your emotions on a roller coaster. Many divorces are often triggered by family finances. And divorce is expensive in terms of dollars, family relationships, emotional stability and uncertainty about the future.

As a financial counselor, I strongly recommend pre-divorce counseling. I have worked with divorce attorneys and mediators of divorce to achieve divorces less costly and with less acrimony, less stress and less time to bring closure.

How long does a divorce take? The answer is: As long as the money last. It's amazing how quickly closure occurs once the money runs out.

My observation in regard to mediated divorces and their results is that, most often, the cost is lower and the time is shorter. The decree will address the issues and accomplish the desired results, provided the parties can sit down and intelligently come to agreement without allowing their emotions to disrupt the sanity needed to achieve a reasonable and acceptable document–one attorneys can represent and courts can accept. However, if the terms of the decree are violated, the only recourse is then to return to court. And the judges and attorneys get involved again.

This opens old wounds and costs more precious time and money.

Stand Up or Bend Over

I have seen pre-divorce planning address the issues—particularly in the financial area—that can prevent post-decree activity and costs. Principle areas of concern are usually credit cards, vehicle titles and some other loans. Other debt that is jointly held needs to be addressed as well. With some planning and specific direction before the divorce, common problems can be avoided, as can a lot of post-decree expense. Cell phone contracts, club memberships and timeshare contracts are additional items that must be addressed if they are jointly held. Separate these issues before the case is finalized, and you will again avoid much post-decree anger, cost and frustration.

STAND UP!
PLAN AHEAD & AVOID MORE PROBLEMS

INTERNAL REVENUE SERVICE (IRS)

There is nothing that strikes fear in the hearts of men like the ETERNAL REVENUE SERVICE. They never go away. They seem to epitomize the ever-present, everlasting and far reaching arm of the government

That said, I have to admit I know some actual stories that demonstrate the IRS has a heart.

The first rule in this game is: Do not ignore them. Talk to them. Tell them the truth. However, the "don't ask, don't tell" axiom remains appropriate.

I want to share a story of a couple that incurred a tax liability for the loss of their home in foreclosure before the law was changed relative to the capital gains tax.

How to Stand Up

An installment payment plan was established and, in the process, it was necessary to review the plan with the IRS each year and make appropriate adjustments. One year I was going through the review with an IRS agent and we came to the rent payment. The agent said the amount was beyond the norm for that zip code and would not be allowed. I protested that position but quickly lost the argument. When we came to the car payment, I told the agent that the car was now paid for. The agent immediately and emphatically said, "Sir, they have a car payment." There was a hesitation as I caught the message of the agent. They were giving back what they took from the rent. AMAZING! The IRS has a heart. Who'd have thought?

STAND UP! BE PATIENT!

BUDGET -
You Can't Change What You Don't Know

The word budget usually resonates negatively with people. For all the good intentions and attempts to develop a budget, most people have given up and continue to fly by the seat of their pants. Please, open your mind and listen up! A budget is necessary and you really need to try one once more.

I want you to understand that a budget can be one of the best tools you have to help you make changes and to achieve your goals. You should start simple. Then build more and more into it. But you need to record everything. It is easy to document the items for which you receive statements or bills. Two of the biggest items in the budget, however, are items I'd bet you don't know the real costs of.

Stand UP or Bend Over

Food and communication expenses top the list. These are big and getting bigger. Here is a clue. Food = groceries + kids lunches + your lunches + fast food + order in + restaurants. Be honest with yourself and figure this one out. You will probably be surprised. If you don't know what you are spending, you will have no basis for, or motivation to change.

I call the second one "the electronic pit." This is made up of cell phones, home phones, cable, internet and any other electronic/entertainment costs you incur. Take a thorough look at this area and ask the tough questions. Shop for better plans. Place some limits on your usage. Demand some accountability from all the participants. These are lifestyle issues and maybe some adjustments in priorities should be considered.

You must track all spending for thirty days to even begin to get a handle on what is really happening. You should create a budget that accurately reflects or represents your family's real lifestyle and actual activities.

Suggestion: Do not include gifts, clothes, home repairs or auto repairs, as these items should not be occurring every month, and therefore should come out of the mythical category called savings.

For more information and detailed instruction on budget building and managing, visit minutemanfinancial.com, where you will find a class that will lead you by the hand though the process, removing much of the fear about using a budget. BUDGET is not to be equated with financial bondage. A budget is actually your roadmap to financial freedom.

STAND UP: START BUDGETING

How to Stand Up

MIRACLES DO HAPPEN

This case involved a couple with two young children and an aged father who was dying of cancer. The husband had been self-employed, but the SBA had just padlocked his business. Now he was unemployed. The wife was working but did not earn very much. They had a home with a mortgage, some equity, a $200,000 SBA loan and substantial credit card debt, along with other miscellaneous debt including $43,000 owed to the IRS. A sad situation.

We went to the IRS office and were assigned an agent that appeared to be ten months pregnant. I was encouraged when she said she would like to close the case before she left on maternity leave. We supplied all the requested documents and information. During the second meeting, the agent said this case would be closed and done. Debt forgiven. I requested a letter be sent stating the decision. She said they don't do that. I suggested that if I sent a letter stating the decision and they did not respond to the contrary, the deal would be sealed. She smiled and nodded affirmative. Wow, step one completed. $43,000 of forgiveness.

Next was to have the client file a Chapter Seven bankruptcy to wipe out all the unsecured debt. That was completed in the normal timeframe and appropriately discharged. This left the house and the SBA to deal with.

Stand Up or Bend Over

The final step was to sell the house. I recommended they list their home "by owner" so as to preserve as much of any proceeds as possible. This was during less troubled times for real estate and an offer came quickly. And it was for cash. I immediately called the SBA and proposed a 5% settlement on the $200,000 loan balance. Approval was secured in forty-eight hours.

The sale closed with a payment of $10,000 to the SBA and the client walked away debt-free, with a modest check from the remaining equity to restart their lives after this series of miracles. REMEMBER, IF YOU DON'T ASK, YOU DON'T GET!

STAND UP! PLAN AHEAD AND
AVOID MORE PROBLEMS

GET ANOTHER OPINION

A recent case involves a new client with an IRS debt of $50,000, unpaid for over eight years and with no means of paying it. I inquired as to how it came about and briefly looked at their documents. They told me that three CPAs reviewed the case and all three said the amount was correct. I asked if they would object to another review. The client said no. Not being a CPA or an IRS expert, I referred the case to our CPA for review.

During the first visit, in less than two hours, a simple call to the IRS reduced the debt to $3,000. The CPA fee was about $300. Can you imagine the burden that was lifted by STANDING UP?

In all professions there are good, better and best. Some are just plain BAD. The best may cost a little more, but in the end you always save money.

STAND UP! PERSISTENCE PAYS

HOW TO BUY A HOUSE

This is a story of a young married couple with two small children. He was a full-time college student who also worked to support the family. They lived in a mobile home on which they made payments and also paid lot rent. They really wanted to buy a house, but they didn't have any money. Neither of them had a rich uncle or parents to provide financial assistance. This young couple had never bought a house and no one told them how to go about doing it.

They spent most weekends for almost a year going to open houses and looking at homes for sale. The wife suggested they call for an appointment to see a particular house they had noticed on the market for an entire year. The house had been taken in trade by a home builder and he had been unable to sell it. The call was made and the appointment set.

At the appointed hour, they met with an agent at the house. It was a two-bedroom bungalow on a narrow lot, in an established neighborhood with an elementary school one block away. A nice neighborhood with young families and some retired folks. A tour through the house determined that the couple was interested. They told the agent that they didn't have any money and that the only way they could swing the deal was for the seller to reduce the price approximately 10%.

Stand Up or Bend Over

The house was solid and the basement was dry. However, the bathroom needed major work. The buyer told the agent that since the company built houses, they could have their carpenters redo the bath at their expense, including new fixtures. The agent wrote it down. The couple told the agent that since the house needed some additional work and they did not have any money, the seller would have to give them $500 at closing so they could buy materials for the improvements. The agent laughed and thought it was a joke. They told him to write it down. The agent smiled and asked if there was anything else? The couple said they lived in a mobile home and owed money on it. To make the deal work, the construction company would have to take the mobile home for the down payment and pay it off. They also needed to stay in the mobile home after the closing for two months to complete the improvements and the construction company would have to make the payments. By this time the agent said, "I know, just write it down." This completed the terms of the purchase offer. As the agent left he said, "Don't call me."

Two days later, the agent called and said his boss had accepted the entire deal as it had been written.

There are several points to make on this case:.
1. If you don't ask, you don't get.
2. Determine what it takes to make the deal work for you. Then go for it, even if it seems outrageous.
3. What seemed to be a very one-sided deal actually turned out to be of mutual benefit.

The construction company took the mobile home and gutted it so it could be used as an office on their construction site. The time delay to take possession of the mobile home didn't cost them anything. They were also able to cut their losses on a prior trade-in that was costing them money, since the property taxes, insurance and maintenance of the property were ongoing.

STAND UP! BE CREATIVE!

How to Stand Up

RECOVERY - Trials to Triumph

This is another case that incorporates foreclosure, bankruptcy, credit restoration and buying another home. This client came to us with a very stressful financial situation. The wife was very emotional and reacted very badly to any idea of foreclosure or bankruptcy. The woman actually bolted out of the office when we first discussed the concept. She did return after a short while.

The instructions to them were to do three things:
1. Seek out a place to live which would meet their needs, be comfortable and affordable.
2. Tell the landlord the truth about their finances, foreclosure, credit, bankruptcy etc...
3. Have the landlord call me.

They found a five-year-old home on a golf course that was in beautiful condition and rented for $850 less per month than their mortgage had been. They followed the recommended steps and were granted a lease. As soon as their bankruptcy was completed, the credit bureaus were checked out for accuracy and a strategy was implemented to rebuild their credit.

In one year, their credit scores were good and at the end of two years, they were excellent. We were able to get them approved to buy another home two-and-a-half years after the discharge of the bankruptcy, which ran during the final months of the foreclosure.

The people found a very nice place to lease, at a very good price with option to purchase, and ended up with a monthly payment less than half of what they were paying on their foreclosed home.

Stand Up or Bend Over

This is an example of how a client went from trials to triumph in a relatively short timeframe. They landed on their feet financially, emotionally and relationally. Their marriage survived, their finances improved and they are now living proof of the resiliency of the human spirit and a sound financial strategy.

STAND UP! REJOICE IN SUCCESS!

WIPE OUT THE DEBT

I received a call on a Monday morning from one of my clients, a single mom. She had received a collection call on Sunday evening and it was brutal. She was still shook up on Monday morning when she called me. The collector had threatened, intimidated and generally abused the poor woman. I told her to immediately document verbatim what was said, as best she could, and to include the good, the bad and the ugly. I told her to get the material to me as soon as possible. As soon as I had it, I called the creditor and went directly to a supervisor. I told her I would be kind. If she would give me her fax number, I would forward a copy of the client notes. I asked her to review them and call me back at her convenience.

I received a call in about twenty minutes and was greeted by a humble supervisor with an apology and a question. What do you want? I clearly stated that I wanted a letter stating the account is "PAID IN FULL" and that it be reported to the credit bureaus as such. This was done immediately and the case was closed.

Knowledge is power! Accurate notes are also very powerful. Record names, dates and the substance of what transpires. Even if the creditor does not respond appropriately, the documentation will most likely be very convincing to a judge if the case goes that far. You'll be the winner!

STAND UP & WIN!

How to Stand Up

COUPONING

It ain't what it used to be. Couponing has moved into the 21st century. And the internet is the source for how to do it. Clipping coupons and keeping the little pocket device for filing them has become passé.

About three years ago, I saw an article in the paper about a couple of moms who were telling their story about couponing and how they had reduced their food bill substantially. I saved the article and that week I introduced the idea to a new client. I said I didn't know much about it, but that I wanted the woman to take the article and let me know what she thought.

Fast-forward two months when she returned for a follow-up meeting. At the end of the meeting, the woman said she had something to show me. She reached into her purse and pulled out five register receipts from one of the upscale grocery stores in the area. My initial thought was, "Lady, I wanted you to save money." Well, I was about to be educated. The five receipts totaled $240.00 and my client had walked out of the store paying $60.00. That's a whopping 75% savings. I almost fell out of my chair.

The woman had obviously gotten serious about saving money. She proceeded to tell me about the process. I subsequently shared the info with other clients and have had wonderful results. Think about this for a minute. Her savings was not a onetime event. Could you save 50% of what you are presently spending? $200, $300 or $400 per month? That would be a nice piece of change to save, use to accelerate your debt retirement or fund a vacation. LIFE IS CHOICES!

Stand Up or Bend Over

An unforeseen benefit came out of this that proved a beautiful thing. My client knew her daughter was more proficient on the internet and enlisted her to help with the couponing project. The daughter then wanted to go with Mom and help her with shopping. A bonding took place between mother and daughter. It was wonderful–teaching mom the value of including her children in her daily activities, lowering food costs and improving a relationship. Plus, a better inventory in the pantry provided more choices and improved meals. Not bad!

STAND UP & EAT BETTER FOR LESS!

SUGGESTED GUIDELINES

When you are dealing with a creditor, a collector or an attorney, you need to be calm, cool and collected. You will not win if you can't maintain control of yourself, your reactions, your language or your attitude. This is truly where you need to STAND UP on the inside and the outside. Be determined to not let them break you, showing you can beat them at their own game.

1. Do not be fearful of these people.
2. Do not return rudeness with the same. Maintain your cool and maintain control.
3. Do not volunteer information to collectors.
4. Request proof of the debt.
5. Take notes. Name, date and substance of what is said, verbatim if you can
6. Even if you owe the debt, don't acknowledge anything.
7. If this is an old debt, remember there is a statute of limitations that may make it uncollectable.

How to Stand Up

Remember that nearly all people that deal with the granting of credit or the collection of money have all been sent to robot school. This turns them into mindless robots with a script. They are not empowered to make decisions. They may be pleasant but are not programmed to accommodate you. They are not able to solve your problem when you request something outside the guidelines they have been given. They may put you into the mindless and endless phone loop, the "I'll transfer you to someone that can help" routine. Welcome to never-never land!

Fair debt collection practices act stipulations ? ? ? ? ? What they cannot do to you!

STAND UP AND DON'T GET BEAT UP!

IT'S TIME TO GET STARTED!

Congratulations, you have conquered this book. Hopefully you have picked up some nuggets of wisdom to help you navigate the financial paths of your life.

The following pages are provided for you to make notes and help you make this book a companion as you monitor your activities, make changes and constantly move closer to achieving your goals and maintaining your financial freedom.

Take the next step and visit www.standuporbendover.net for financial resources including: online classes, webinars and expert advice. We also recommend subscribing to our personal finance report, "News You Can Use," emailed monthly, including practical knowledge and real-life stories of people just like you, intended to help you stay on course and up-to-date with the changes and challenges of your financial world.

IN CLOSING

The creation of this book has been a joy and a delight. The critical critiques of friends, employees and peers have always inspired me when I needed a little push.

I hope it has provided some insight and nuggets of wisdom for helping you move toward financial freedom.

If you have benefited from the content of these pages, you may be interested to know this is the first of a series of STAND UP OR BEND OVER titles.

They are being developed to bring you more inspirational material and to address additional dimensions of personal finance, relationships and patriotism.

Remember, you were uniquely and beautifully made. Don't let anyone put you in a ticky-tacky box, just because you are supposed to fit their idea that everybody is the same. One-plan-or-strategy-fits-all is not a valid approach to solving your life challenges. Think way outside the box and develop a unique solution to your unique situation. STAND UP, think, educate yourself and take responsibility for you!

I would appreciate your thoughts and comments. Please be kind and post them at www.amazon.com or at www.standuporbendover.net

Thank you for allowing me to be a part of your journey.

Tom Johnson

Notes

CONSUMER BILL OF RIGHTS

If you have been denied credit because of incorrect or incomplete information in a report furnished by a Consumer Reporting Agency, the law grants you certain rights, including the following.

1. The right to request in writing and obtain at no charge, from the agency, upon proper identification, the nature and substance of asked for information (except medical information) contained in the files at the time of the request.

2. The right to request in writing and to obtain from the agency, upon proper identification, the source of all information (except investigative reporting).

3. The name and address of all recipients of an adverse report concerning the consumer given within six months of the date requested, or within two years of the request if the report was given for employment purposes.

4. The right to dispute in writing the information contained in an adverse report about the consumer.

5. The right to request in writing that adverse information believed by the consumer to be incomplete or incorrect, be investigated by the agency (unless the request is frivolous), and if the information is found to be incorrect, or cannot be verified, the right to have the agency remove such information from the consumers file.

6. The right to request in writing and to obtain from the agency a copy of all information on which the consumer has been denied credit, insurance or employment, within 30 days of the consumer's interview. Otherwise, the agency is permitted to charge a reasonable fee for giving the consumer this information.

7. The right to request the agency in writing that it notifies (without charge) those named by the consumer who previously received the incorrect or incomplete information that such information has been deleted from the consumer's file.

8. The right to request the agency in writing to send the consumer's version of the dispute to certain companies for a reasonable fee.

9. The right to have the agency withhold a consumer's report from anyone who under the law does not have a legitimate need for the information.

10. The right to NOT have adverse information reported by the agency after seven years except for bankruptcy, which is ten years.

CASH POOR CREDIT RICH
CPR for Your Financial Freedom

Mr. Johnson's book, "Cash Poor Credit Rich." meets you where you are–depressed, frustrated, angry, hopeless, and the list goes on. Are you facing a loss of income, overwhelming bills, credit card debt or bankruptcy? Is your home only worth half of what you owe on your mortgage? Has your 401k and pension taken major hits in this economy, leaving you with little hope for retirement? It might be time to perform a radical makeover of your financial world and begin to enjoy your life by moving toward FINANCIAL FREEDOM.

No matter how much you make, you don't have enough. Truly, you need CPR for your financial heart. This little, easy-to-read-book and our online video classes can help you make a fresh start. We provide you with the practical, easy-to-understand steps and the tools you will need to makeover your finances and plot a new path toward financial freedom.

This book arms you with the knowledge and resources you need to take the steps to achieve it. "Cash Poor Credit Rich" includes resources on:

- Problem Resolution
- Goal Setting
- Your Credit Report
- Restructuring Your Finances
- Foreclosure Defense
- Building a Budget
- Preservation of Cash
- Bankruptcy
- How to Deal with Creditors

Available at Amazon.com or www.StandUporBendOver.net

Notes

Notes

Notes

Notes